Thanks for Being You

Artwork by

Judy Buswell

H®
HARVEST HOUSE PUBLISHERS
EUGENE, OREGON

Thanks for Being You

Text Copyright © 2006 by Harvest House Publishers
Eugene, Oregon 97402

ISBN=13: 978-0-7369-1797-1
ISBN=10: 0-7369-1797-7
Product #: 6917971

Design and production by Garborg Design Works

Harvest House Publishers has made every effort to trace the ownership of all poems and quotes. In the event of a question arising from the use of a poem or quote, we regret any error made and will be pleased to make the necessary correction in future editions of this book.

Printed in China

06 07 08 09 10 11 12 / LP / 10 9 8 7 6 5 4 3 2 1

To:

_____

With Love,

_____

Life is so much better with you in it.
Thanks for being you!

I have learned that to have a good friend is the purest of all
Gods gifts, for it is a love that has no exchange of payment.

FRANCES FARMER

Friendship only is, indeed,
genuine when two friends,
without speaking a word
to each other, can nevertheless
find happiness in being together.

GEORGE EBER

*You remind me of what's
really important in life:
friends, best friends.*

FANNIE FLAGG
THE WHISTLE STOP CAFÉ

4

Are we not like two volumes of one book?

Marceline Desbordes-Valmore

5

Yes'm, old friends is always best, 'less you can catch a new one that's fit to make an old one out of.

SARAH ORNE JEWETT

Friendships aren't perfect,
and yet they are very precious.
For me, not expecting
perfection all in one
place was a great release.

LETTY COTTIN POGREBIN

Thank you for your letter; it was
as pleasant as a quiet chat, as
welcome as spring showers, as
reviving as a friend's visit...

A LETTER FROM CHARLOTTE BRONTË TO HER FRIEND

*T*o think that her friend
loved her in return brought a
sensation of deep happiness,
not unmixed with gratitude.

DINAH MARIA MULOCK CRAIK

*M*arianna has lived such a
private, interior life that, as
much as she likes Constance,
she still cannot reveal herself.
It is not her way, and she
senses that Constance is the
only woman in the quilting
circle who would understand
that because Constance is
like her in that respect.

WHITNEY OTTO
HOW TO MAKE AN AMERICAN QUILT

The secret to
friendship is being
a good listener.

9

True happiness

consists not in

the multitude

of friends, but

in the worth

and choice.

BEN JOHNSON

I consider you

as a friend,

who will take me

just as I am,

good, or bad,

or indifferent.

JAMES BOSWELL

11

We must love our friends for their sakes rather than for our own; we must look at their truth to themselves, full as much as to themselves.

CHARLOTTE BRONTË

In real friendship the judgment, the genius, the prudence of each party become the common property of both.

MARIA EDGEWORTH

*O*ne is taught by experience to put a premium on those few people who can appreciate you for what you are.

GAIL GOODWIN

13

*M*y second friendship...was formed in Lawrence. I was not more than ten years old when I met this new friend, but the memory of her in after-years, and the impression she had made on my susceptible young mind, led me first into the ministry, next into medicine, and finally into suffrage-work. Living next door to us, on Prospect Hill, was a beautiful and mysterious woman. All we children knew of her was that she was a vivid and romantic figure, who seemed to have no friends and of whom our elders spoke in whispers or not at all. To me she was a princess in a fairy-tale...

Very soon she noticed me. Possibly she saw the adoration in my childish eyes. She began to nod and smile at me, and then to speak to me...and a strange friendship began and developed between the woman of the town and the little girl she loved. Some of those visits I remember as vividly as if I had made them yesterday...While I was with her, my hostess became a child again, and we played together like children. She had wonderful toys for me, and pictures and books; but the thing I loved best of all and played with for hours was a little stuffed hen which she told me had been her dearest treasure when she was a child at home. She had also a stuffed puppy, and she once mentioned that those two things alone were left of her life as a little girl. Besides the toys and books and pictures, she gave me ice-cream and cake, and told me fairy-tales. She had a wonderful understanding of what a child likes.

ANNA HOWARD SHAW
THE STORY OF A PIONEER

Though love be deeper, friendship is more wide.

CORINNE ROOSEVELT ROBINSON

Let us enjoy each other and be sure
That no rainburst or seas or seastorm lure
Us to separation before our lives end...

LOUISE LABE

What a luxury it
was to spend time with
old friends with whom
it was okay to talk
about nothing much.

LISA ALTHER

Oh, the comfort, the inexpressible comfort of feeling safe
with a person, having neither to weigh thoughts, nor measure
words, but pouring them all right out, just as they are—chaff
and grain together—certain that a faithful hand will take and
sift them, keep what is worth keeping and with the breath of
kindness blow the rest away.

DINAH MARIA MULOCK CRAIK

A Friend or Two

There's all of pleasure and all of peace
In a friend or two;
And all your troubles may find release
Within a friend or two;
It's in the grip of the sleeping hand
On native soil or in alien land,
But the world is made—do you understand—
Of a friend or two.

A song to sing, and a crust to share
With a friend or two;
A smile to give and a grief to bear
With a friend or two;
A road to walk and a goal to win,
An inglenook to find comfort in,
The gladdest hours that we know begin
With a friend or two.

A little laughter, perhaps some tears
With a friend or two;
The days, the weeks, and the months and years
With a friend or two;
A vale to cross and a hill to climb,
A mock at age and a jeer at time—
The prose of life takes the lilt of rhyme
With a friend or two.

The brother-soul and the brother-heart
Of a friend or two;
Make us drift on from the crowd apart,
With a friend or two;
For come days happy or come days sad,
We count no hours but the ones made glad
By the hale good times we have ever had
With a friend or two.

Then brim the goblet and quaff the toast
To a friend or two;
For glad the man who can always boast
Of a friend or two;
But fairest sight is a friendly face,
The blithest tread is a friendly pace,
And heaven will be a better place
For a friend or two.

WILBUR D. NESBIT

I awoke this morning with devout thanksgiving for my friends, the old and the new. Shall I not call God the Beautiful, who daily showeth himself so to me in his gifts? I chide society, I embrace solitude, and yet I am not so ungrateful as not to see the wise, the lovely, and the noble-minded, as from time to time they pass my gate. Who hears me, who understands me, becomes mine,—a possession for all time.

RALPH WALDO EMERSON

A friend is someone we turn to,
When our spirits need a lift.
A friend is someone we treasure,
For our friendship is a gift.
A friend is someone who fills our lives,
With beauty, joy, and grace.
And makes the world we live in,
a better and happier place.

AUTHOR UNKNOWN

20

Friendship without self-interest is one of

There comes that mysterious meeting in life when someone acknowledges who we are and what we can be, igniting the circuits of our highest potential.

RUSTY BERKUS

Blessed are they who have the gift of making friends, for it is one of God's best gifts. It involves many things, but above all, the power of going out of one's self, and appreciating whatever is noble and loving in another.

THOMAS HUGHES

the rare and beautiful things in life.

JAMES FRANCIS BYRNES

23

Friendship... is a union of spirits, a marriage of hearts, and the bond thereto virtue.

WILLIAM PENN

By friendship you mean the greatest love, the greatest usefulness, the most open communication, the noblest sufferings, the severest truth, the heartiest counsel, and the greatest union of minds of which brave men and women are capable.

JEREMY TAYLOR

My friend, the thought of you will be a new motive for every right action. What wealth it is to have such friends that we cannot think of them without elevation.

HENRY DAVID THOREAU

A reassuring presence.

A light when times are dark.

A hand reaching out.

Is what friendship is about.

AUTHOR UNKNOWN

Sometimes people come into your life and you know right away they are meant to be there; they serve some sort of purpose, teach you a lesson, or help you figure out who you are.

AUTHOR UNKNOWN

No friendship is an accident.

O. HENRY

27

*I*n friendship...we think we have chosen our peers. In reality, a few years difference in the date of our births, a few more miles between certain houses, the choice of one university instead of another, posting to different regiments, the accident of a topic being raised or not raised at a first meeting—any of these chances might have kept us apart. But...there are, strictly speaking, no chances.

A secret Master of Ceremonies has been at work... The Friendship is not a reward for our discrimination and good taste in finding one another out. It is the instrument by which God reveals to each the beauties of all others. They are no greater than the beauties of a thousand other men; by Friendship God opens our eyes to them. They are, like all beauties, derived from Him, and then, in a good Friendship, increased by time through the Friendship itself, so that it is His instrument for creation as well as for revealing.

C.S. LEWIS
THE FOUR LOVES

$\mathcal{A}$s the two boys walked sorrowing along, they made a new compact to stand by each other and be brothers and never separate till death relieved them of their troubles.

MARK TWAIN
THE ADVENTURES OF TOM SAWYER

Think where man's glory most begins and ends.

And say my glory was I had such friends.

WILLIAM BUTLER YEATS

$\mathcal{F}$riendship is like an exquisite jewel, forged and clarified by the fires of life. If we observe it carefully, we see a myriad of facets in its ever-changing face; the world reflected in it, ourselves reflected in it. What a precious thing! Cherish it always...

KIM JACOBS

Man's best support
is a very dear friend.
CICERO

The mind never unbends itself so agreeably as in the conversation of a well-chosen friend. There is indeed no blessing of life that is any way comparable to the enjoyment of a discreet and virtuous friend. It eases and unloads the mind, clears and improves the understanding, engenders thought and knowledge, animates virtue and good resolutions, soothes and allays the passions, and finds employment for most of the vacant hours of life.

JOSEPH ADDISON

33

Friends are the sunshine of life.

JOHN HAY

The pleasure of your company is a many-sided affair. It includes the pleasure of seeing you, the pleasure of hearing you talk, the drama of watching your actions, your likes and dislikes and adventures; the pleasure of hunting you up in your haunts, and the delicate flattery we feel when you hunt us up in ours.

AUTHOR UNKNOWN

To have a good

friend is one of the

highest delights of

life; to be a good

friend is one of

the noblest and

most difficult

undertakings.

AUTHOR UNKNOWN

*Friendship is a strong
and habitual inclination
in two persons to
promote the good and
happiness in one another.*

EUSTACE BUDGELL

A true friend is the gift of God, and he

only who made hearts can unite them.

ROBERT SOUTH

Perhaps the most delightful friendships are those in which there is much agreement, much disputation, and yet more personal liking.

GEORGE ELIOT

Of all the things which wisdom provides to make life entirely happy, much the greatest is the possession of friendship.

EPICURUS

Congeniality, when once established between two kindred spirits or in a group, is the most carefree of human relationships. It is effortless, like purring. It is a basic theme in friendship...

FRANCES LESTER WARNER

39

Wake up with a smile

and go after life...

Live it, enjoy it, taste it,

smell it, feel it.

JOE KNAPP

A man with few friends is only half-developed; there are whole sides of his nature which are locked up and have never been expressed. He cannot unlock them himself, he cannot even discover them; friends alone can stimulate him and open him.

RANDOLPH BOURNE

Thus nature has no love for solitude, and always leans, as it were, on some support; and the sweetest support is found in the most intimate friendship.

CICERO

42

Friends are the most important ingredient in the recipe of life.

AUTHOR UNKNOWN

So long as we love, we serve;
so long as we are loved by others,
I should say that we are almost
indispensable; and no man is
useless while he has a friend.

ROBERT LOUIS STEVENSON

*Verily great grace may
go with a little gift;
and precious are all things
that come from friends.*

THEOCRITUS

Friendship is something you can't buy and can't command, but you can lose. So it must be refreshed. At all times, and before it's too late, it needs refreshment... What matters is the intent—the intent to keep alive something worthy and mutual. This happens when people remember each other, cultivate each other, meet each other a little more than halfway. Such are the ways in which friendship may be shared.

Nothing on earth is more important, for, just as it has been said that "to lose a friend is to die a little," so the reverse is also true, and when you keep a friend you add something to the richness and the worth of life.

FRANK V. MORLEY

O the world is wide and the world is grand,

And there's little or nothing new.

But it's sweetest thing is the grip of the hand

Of the friend who's tried and true.

AUTHOR UNKNOWN

45

A friendship can weather most things and thrive in thin soil, but it needs just a little mulch of letters and phone calls and small, silly presents every so often—just to save it from drying out completely.

PAM BROWN

To be a good friend..." How simple it sounds—just five short words. Yet how much they represent! Think how much it could mean, a flowing out of new forces of friendship from person to person, and eventually from land to land.

ROBERT HARDY ANDREWS

Your words came just when needed.
Like a breeze
Blowing and bringing from the
Wide soft sea
Some cooling spray, to meadow
Scorched with heat
And choked with dust and clouds
Of sifted sand...
So words of thine came over
Miles to me,
Fresh from the mighty sea, a
True friend's heart,
And brought me hope, strength,
And swept away
The dusty webs that human
Spiders spun
Across my path, Friend—and
The word means much—
So few there are who reach
like thee, a hand...

ELLA WHEELER COX